THE CAST LIST
DUKE OF INCONSTANCY
VARIOUS UNNAMED GENTLEMEN
HUSBAND to the CREATING PRINCESS
UNFORTUNATE DUTCHESS, and her WOMAN
CREATING PRINCESS, and her WOMAN
COMICAL DUTCHESS, and her WOMAN
VARIOUS ATTENDANTS
LADY TRUE HONOUR
MADAM INQUIRER
TWO or THREE BURGERS WIVES
TWO SCRIVENERS WIVES
VARIOUS UNNAMED WOMEN

ACT I

SCENE I

Enter the **UNFORTUNATE DUTCHESS**, and her **WOMAN**.

WOMAN
Dear Madam, why doth your Highness weep?

UNFORTUNATE DUTCHESS
As fear frights tears from the Eyes, so grief doth send them forth.

WOMAN
Why should your Highness grieve?

UNFORTUNATE DUTCHESS
Have I not cause, when I am married to a person which doth not love, but rather hate me?

WOMAN
Certainly he hath reason to love you, and he were worse than a Devil if he should hate you; as first to love you for your virtue and sweet disposition; next for the honour, dignity, and Kingdome, he hath got by his marring you: for he hath no right to the Dukedome but by your Highness, and by your Highness he is become an absolute Prince, and injoyes a rich Kingdome.

UNFORTUNATE DUTCHESS
But he hath taken the power from me, and strives to disposess of me of my right.

WOMAN
He cannot, the Kingdome will never suffer him, for your title is so just, as he can make no pretence to disposess your Highness from your Princely Throne.

UNFORTUNATE DUTCHESS
But I being his Wife, he takes the power of a Husband, and by that power, the power of my Kingdome, and those that have the power can frame their titles as they please, none dare oppose them.

WOMAN
The truth is, Madam, that might overcomes right.

[Exeunt.

SCENE II

Enter **TWO GENTLEMEN**

FIRST GENTLEMEN
The Factions and divisions that are in this Kingdome will be a means to deliver it into the power of the Enemy.

SECOND GENTLEMEN
This Duke is young, wild, deboist and inconstant, wherefore there is but little hopes it should be better governed.

FIRST GENTLEMEN
But the Dutchess who is the true owner of it, is discreet, wise, and virtuous, and having more years than he, she might help to rule and order state affairs.

SECOND GENTLEMEN
But neither her discretion, wisdome, nor virtue hath power, for marriage hath inthralled her, for she is become her Husbands Slave, who ought to be his Soveraign, but he laughs and doth despise her, because she is somewhat elder than himself.

FIRST GENTLEMEN
Heaven will revenge her wrongs.

[Exeunt.

SCENE III

The Apocriphal Ladies by Margaret Cavendish

Margaret Lucas Cavendish, Duchess of Newcastle-upon-Tyne was born in 1623 in Colchester, Essex into a family of comfortable means.

As the youngest of eight children she spent much time with her siblings. Margaret had no formal education but she did have access to scholarly libraries and tutors, although she later said the children paid little attention to the tutors, who were there 'rather for formality than benefit'.

From an early age Margaret was already assembling her thoughts for future works despite the then conditions of society that women did not partake in public authorship. For England it was also a time of Civil War. The Royalists were being pushed back and Parliamentary forces were in the ascendancy.

Despite these obvious dangers, when Queen Henrietta Maria was in Oxford, Margaret asked her mother for permission to become one of her Ladies-in-waiting. She was accepted and, in 1644, accompanied the Queen into exile in France. This took her away from her family for the first time.

Despite living at the Court of the young King Louis XIV, life for the young Margaret was not what she expected. She was far from her home and her confidence had been replaced by shyness and difficulties fitting in to the grandeur of her surroundings and the eminence of her company.

Margaret told her mother she wanted to leave the Court. Her mother was adamant that she should stay and not disgrace herself by leaving. She provided additional funds for her to make life easier. Margaret remained. It was now also that she met and married William Cavendish who, at the time, was the Marquis of Newcastle (and later Duke). He was also 30 years her senior and previously married with two children.

As Royalists, a return to life in England was not yet possible. They would remain in exile in Paris, Rotterdam and Antwerp until the restoration of the crown in 1660 although Margaret was able to return for attention to some estate matters.

Along with her husband's brother, Sir Charles Cavendish, she travelled to England after having been told that her husband's estate (taken from him due to his being a royalist) was to be sold and that she, as his wife, would receive some benefit of the sale. She received nothing. She left England to be with her husband again.

The couple were devoted to each other. Margaret wrote that he was the only man she was ever in love with, loving him not for title, wealth or power, but for merit, justice, gratitude, duty, and fidelity. She also relied upon him for support in her career. The marriage provided no children despite efforts made by her physician to overcome her inability to conceive.

Margaret's first book, 'Poems and Fancies', was published in 1653; it was a collection of poems, epistles and prose pieces which explores her philosophical, scientific and aesthetic ideas.

For a woman at this time writing and publishing were avenues they had great difficulty in pursuing. Added to this was Margaret's range of subjects. She wrote across a number of issues including gender, power, manners, scientific method, and philosophy.

She always claimed she had too much time on her hands and was therefore able to indulge her love of writing. As a playwright she produced many works although most are as closet dramas. (This is a play not intended to be performed onstage, but instead read by a solitary reader or perhaps out loud in a small group. For Margaret the rigours of exile, her gender and Cromwell's closing of the theatres mean this was her early vehicle of choice and, despite these handicaps, she became one of the most well-known playwrights in England)

Her utopian romance, 'The Blazing World', (1666) is one of the earliest examples of science fiction. Margaret also published extensively in natural philosophy and early modern science; at least a dozen books.

She was the first woman to attend a meeting at Royal Society of London in 1667 and she criticized and engaged with members and philosophers Thomas Hobbes, René Descartes, and Robert Boyle.

Margaret was always defended against any criticism by her husband and he also contributed to some of her works. She also gives him credit as her writing tutor.

Perhaps a little strangely she said her ambition despite her shyness, was to have everlasting fame. During her career, from the mid 1650's until her death, she was prolific. In recent decades her work has undergone a resurgence of interest propelled mainly by her ground-breaking attitude and accomplishments in those male straitened times.

Margaret Cavendish died on 15th December 1673 and was buried at Westminster Abbey.

Index of Contents

Enter the **DUKE OF INCONSTANCY**, and a **GENTLEMEN**.

DUKE OF INCONSTANCY
Have you been with the Lady I sent you to?

GENTLEMEN
Yes.

DUKE OF INCONSTANCY
And doth she lissen to Loves Sute?

GENTLEMEN
She seems well pleased to hear her Beauty praised, but will not hear of Amorous imbracements as yet.

DUKE OF INCONSTANCY
But it is a good Omen when as a Lady will nimblingly bite at a bait of flattery; but did you see her Husband?

GENTLEMEN
No Sir.

DUKE OF INCONSTANCY
Well, you must go again, and present her with a Letter, and a present from me; for Ladies must be plied though they deny, yet most do yield upon a treaty, they cannot long hold out loves fierce assaults.

GENTLEMEN
Indeed the Female Sex is tender and weak, although they are delicate and sweet.

DUKE OF INCONSTANCY
They are false and oft betray themselves.

[Exeunt.

SCENE IV

Enter the **UNFORTUNATE DUTCHESS**, and her **WOMAN**; then enters another as running in haste.

WOMAN
O Madam, Madam, news is come that the Enemy hath got into the heart of the Kingdome; wherefore sweet Lady fly, for they will possess themselves of this City soon.

UNFORTUNATE DUTCHESS
I will not fly, for I cannot meet a worse Enemy than the Duke himself, should worse than Mankind Conquer it; but I wish my Sister were safe.

WOMAN
The young Princess I hear is fled to the Dukes Brother.

UNFORTUNATE DUTCHESS
I am glad of it, for he is discreetly temperate, although his Brother is not.

[Exeunt.

SCENE V

Enter the **DUKE OF INCONSTANCY**, and a **GENTLEMEN**.

GENTLEMEN
Sir, what will your Highness do?

DUKE OF INCONSTANCY
I will go and oppose the Enemy.

GENTLEMEN
Alass Sir you have no forces to oppose them withall, you may go to be destroyed, but not to destroy; wherefore you with your small forces had better fly than fight.

DUKE OF INCONSTANCY
Whither shall I go?

GENTLEMEN
To any Prince that will receive you into pay, by which you may maintain your self, and live with some respect and fame abroad, though you have lost your Kingdome; whereas if you stay, you will lose your self and Kingdome too.

DUKE OF INCONSTANCY
Your Counsel I will take.

GENTLEMEN
But what will your Highness do with your Dutchess?

DUKE OF INCONSTANCY
Let her do what she will with her self, I care not now, for since her Kingdome is lost, I have no use of her.

GENTLEMEN
Not as concerning the Kingdome Sir, but yet she is your Highnesses Wife, and as a Husband you ought to regard her.

DUKE OF INCONSTANCY
She will follow me, for Wives stick so close to their Husbands as they cannot be shaken off.

[Exeunt.

Enter the **CREATING PRINCESS**, and her **WOMAN**.

WOMAN
Pray Madam do not marry so much below your self.

CREATING PRINCESS
Why? what matter whom I marry, since I can create my Husband to Honour.

WOMAN
But Madam, that Honour will do him no good, nor will it take off your disgrace; for none will give your Husband, if he be an inferiour person, the Place and Respect that is due to Great Princes Titles.

CREATING PRINCESS
No, but he shall take Place, and my Servants shall give him the Respect and Homage that is due to great Titles: For I will make him a Prince; and who dare call him any other, but Prince?

WOMAN
There is none will call him Prince, unless your own Servants; and none will give him Place, that are above the degree of his Birth: no, nor he durst not take it of Gallant Noble Men; for if he offers thereat, they will beat him back, and force him to give way, and to be only a Prince in his own House, and not abroad, is no better than to be a Farmer, nay, a Cobler, or a Tayler, or any the like are Kings in their own Houses, although they be but thatch'd, if they have but a Servant subject, or Subject Servant.

CREATING PRINCESS
Well, say what you will, I will make him a Prince.

[Exeunt.

Enter the **DUKE OF INCONSTANCY**, and a **GENTLEMEN**.

GENTLEMEN
Sir, doth not your Highness hear that your Dutchess is gone with your Enemies into the Countrey?

DUKE OF INCONSTANCY
Yes, and though I might curse my Enemies for dispossessing me of the Kingdom I injoyed, yet I give them thanks for carrying my Wife away with them: for now I have more room and liberty to Wooe and Court my Mistress.

[Enter another **GENTLEMAN**.

FIRST GENTLEMEN
Sir, the Lady Beauties Husband's dead.

DUKE OF INCONSTANCY
So I perceive Fortune will be my Friend some waies, although she is my Foe other waies: for she will Crown me with Love, although she uncrowns me with Power: wherefore return presently back to my Mistriss, and tell her, that now her Husband is dead, and my Wife gone into another Country, We may marry.

[Exeunt.

FIRST GENTLEMEN
But your Highness cannot marry, as long as the Dutchess is alive.

DUKE OF INCONSTANCY
I mean to be like the Great Turk, have many Wives.

FIRST GENTLEMEN
Why, the Great Turk hath but one chief Wife, the rest are but as Concubines: for only the Sons of that chief Queen shall be Successors to the Emperor, unless she hath none, neither can his other Children inherit,unless he be Right and Lawfull Emperor: So, that unless your Highness had been Duke by Inheritance, as an Inhereditary Duke, no Children, by any other Lady, can be Inheritors, nor indeed Princes, unless they were begot on the Right Owner to that Title.

DUKE OF INCONSTANCY
Well, since I have no Power, but only an empty Title, I cannot disadvantage my self, or children: for I have no children as yet, and I have neither Power, nor Kingdom now: Wherefore, if I can injoy her upon these tearms, as the name of Wife, it will be well.

GENTLEMEN
But Sir, this part of the World allows but of one wife, wherefore if you should marry this Lady, the Clergy will excommunicate you, as an Adulterer, and the Lady, as an Adulteress, out of the Church.

DUKE OF INCONSTANCY
I had rather be in the Ladies bed, than in the Church: But I have money, although I have lost my Dukedom, and that will help me.

GENTLEMEN
But not make your Marriage lawfull.

DUKE OF INCONSTANCY
I care not; for if the marrying, and the name of wife will satisfie the Lady, I care not whether it be Good or Bad, Lawfull or unlawfull, Wife or Concubine, 'tis all one to me; for I will marry a hundred women, if they will marry me, and let me lye with them.

[Exeunt.

Enter the **UNFORTUNATE DUTCHESS**, and her **WOMAN**

WOMAN
Your Highness bears afflictions more couragiously than I thought your Highness would have done.

UNFORTUNATE DUTCHESS
Truly, I find I am more happy since I am amongst my Enemies (if they may be termed so) than I was in my own Country with an unkind Husband: for they allow me a Noble and Princely Pension: and I live Free, Easily and Peaceably, which I did not before.

WOMAN
I hear your Sister is marryed to the Dukes Brother.

UNFORTUNATE DUTCHESS
I wish she may be more happy with her Husband, than I have been with mine.

WOMAN
If they have Children, and your Highness none, they will be Heirs to the Dukedom.

UNFORTUNATE DUTCHESS
They will so, but there is no Dukedom now to heir, 'tis made now a Province.

WOMAN
But times may change.

[Exeunt.

Enter the **COMICAL DUTCHESS**, and her **WOMAN**.

WOMAN
Now you are an absolute Dutchess, you must carry your self in State, and live Magnificently, like as an Absolute Princess as you are.

COMICAL DUTCHESS
Yes, but it is a great affliction for the Duke and I to be banished, and driven out of our Kingdom.

WOMAN

Alass Madam, great Princes have many times great misfortunes; but you must bear your misfortunes with a Princely magnaminity.

COMICAL DUTCHESS
But if I have Children, alass what shall they do?

WOMAN
But those that did never injoy the possession, cannot repine, nor grieve for the loss.

COMICAL DUTCHESS
You say true.

[Exeunt.

SCENE X

Enter the **CREATING PRINCESS**, and her **WOMAN**

WOMAN
Pray Madam do not marry so meanly, for you cannot intitle him a Prince.

CREATING PRINCESS
Well, well, say what you will, I will make him a Prince; for why may not I as well make my Husband lawfully a Prince, as well as the Duke of Inconstancy makes the Lady Beauty a Dutchess, and yet hath another Wife?

WOMAN
Introth it will be just like a poor Begger Woman in Engl. being mad she said she was Queen Elizabeth of England, and all the Boys, Girls, and Common people would run after her, and call her Queen Elizabeth in sport and jest; the like was a poor mad Begger Man in France, which said he was King Henry the 4th. of France; but the only difference will be, that you and the Comical Dutchess have means and wealth enough to live in Principy, and they had none, but were so poor they were forced to beg, so could not Act their parts.

CREATING PRINCESS
You are a bold rude wench, therefore get you out of my service.

WOMAN
Truly I would not stay in it if I might, for I should be ashamed.

[Exeunt.

SCENE XI

Enter the **UNFORTUNATE DUTCHESS**, and her **WOMAN**

WOMAN
Madam, doth your Highness here of the Apocriphal Dutchess?

UNFORTUNATE DUTCHESS
What Apocriphal Dutchess?

WOMAN
Why the Duke hath married another Lady.

UNFORTUNATE DUTCHESS
That he cannot, untill I dye, 'tis true a Mistriss may take the name of a Wife, but cannot possess the right of a Wife.

WOMAN
She will be as a Dutchess in a Play, she will only act the part of greatness.

UNFORTUNATE DUTCHESS
Indeed most Stage-Players are Curtizans.

WOMAN
And most Curtizans are good Actors.

UNFORTUNATE DUTCHESS
I make no question but she will now have enough Spectators.

WOMAN
But I hope they will hiss her from off the Stage.

[Exeunt.

SCENE XII

Enter the **CREATING PRINCESS**, and her **HUSBAND**.

CREATING PRINCESS
Have I married you who was a mean fellow, and have not I made you a Prince, and you to deny to pay my Debts?

HUSBAND
But I thought you would have rather inrich me, than have made me poorer than I was.

CREATING PRINCESS

Have I not inriched you with Titles? do not all my Servants call you Prince? and do not all the Trades-men where we buy all our Commodities, when they come to our Palace do the same, call you Prince, and doe you reverence?

HUSBAND
Yes for hopes of gain.

CREATING PRINCESS
I am sure you will gain little reputation or respect if you carry your self so sneakingly as you do, whereas you should carry your self like a Prince, bravely.

HUSBAND
But when all our money is gone we shall be but poor Princes: I had better have keep to my Trade than to have been a Prince, where if I had I should have been rich, now I shall be a Beggar.

CREATING PRINCESS
You are so mean a fellow as you cannot be sensible of the honour and dignity I have bestowed upon you.

[Exeunt.

SCENE XIII

Enter the **COMICAL DUTCHESS** big with Child, she sits under her Canopy in a Chair of state, her **ATTENDANTS** by her wait on her.

FIRST ATTENDANT
All the great Ladies are so envious at your Highness, as there will none of them come neer you.

COMICAL DUTCHESS
I like the Company of Bourgers Wives better, for they are my Slaves.

SECOND ATTENDANT
Yes Madam, but your Highness is forced I think to present them with some presents now and then; for the World is so wicked, that they will not give true honour it's due, unless they are bribed.

THIRD ATTENDANT
You say true, but men will give Ladies their due right.

FOURTH ATTENDANT
Yes, men are more generous and bountifull to Ladies; but yet they must be bribed with hopes of obtaining some favours, otherwayes, I fear me they would be as reserved, and retired from your Highnesses Court as the great Ladies are.

COMICAL DUTCHESS
I wonder they should, I being an absolute Princess.

SECOND ATTENDANT
Yes, but since your Titles, Rights and Marriage is renounced against, they are not so civil, dutifull, and obedient as they were, not considering as they ought to do, that right cannot be renounced against.

THIRD ATTENDANT
But her Highness doth shew them their error, and that she shews them it cannot be taken from her; for she keeps the same State she did, and is as Merry, Gay and Frollick, to let the World see; she understands her own Greatness best.

FIRST ATTENDANT
But yet there are but few of any Nation, but the inferior sort, that come to her Highness Court, unless it be the Red Oker Knights and Ladies, and if it were not for them, this Court would be empty.

COMICAL DUTCHESS
Indeed I am obliged to them more than any other Nation, for they give me all the due Respects and Homage to my Greatness; for which I love that Nation very well.

SECOND ATTENDANT
You have reason, but I do observe there is nothing doth keep up a Court more than Dancing, and several sorts and kinds of merry pastime; for wheresoever there is Dancing and Sport, Company will flock together.

THIRD ATTENDANT
You say true.

COMICAL DUTCHESS
I find my self full of pain; I believe I shall fall in Labour.

FOURTH ATTENDANT
I hope then we shall have a young Prince, or Princess soon.

[Exeunt.

SCENE XIV

Enter **THREE GENTLEMEN**

FIRST GENTLEMEN
I saw Prince Shaddow.

SECOND GENTLEMEN
What Prince is he?

FIRST GENTLEMEN
Why he is the Creating Princess's Husband, who made him a Prince.

THIRD GENTLEMEN

I thought no women could give Title to their Husbands, unless they had been Soveraigns.

SECOND GENTLEMEN

O yes, all women can give their Husbands Titles, if they please.

THIRD GENTLEMEN

What Title?

SECOND GENTLEMEN

Why the title of Cuckolds.

FIRST GENTLEMEN

Indeed most women do magnifie their Husbands by those Titles.

SECOND GENTLEMEN

But let me tell you, that those women that have Inheritary Honours, although not Soveraigns, may indue their Husbands with the same Honour: but it is not generally so; but his Children begot on her are indued, and not the Husband, yet some Husbands are. As for Example; a Lord, Vicount, Earl, Marquiss, Duke, King, or Emperor, if the Honour, as Title, goeth to the Female, for default of a Male, in some Nations their Husbands are indued with their Titles, but not commonly known to be so in England; as a Wife with her Husband, which is only during life, and not Inheredytary: but if their Titles are only during life, and not Inheredytary, it cannot derive to another, that is not a Successor: for Inheredytary Honour goe like Intailed Lands, it goeth only to the next Heir; but those that are the dignified, are like those that have Joynters, or Annuities for life; so when a Husband receives a Dignity from a Wife, or a Wife from a Husband, it is but so much Honour for life.

FIRST GENTLEMEN

But if they have Children, those Children inherit the Honour.

SECOND GENTLEMEN

Yes, as having a right from that Parent that is the Dignifyer, but if there be none of the line of the Dignifyer, the Honour dies, neither is the root of the Honour left to any more than one: for though the branches of Honour spread to all the Children, yet the root remains but with one: For, say a King have many Children, they are all Princes, but yet there can be but one that can inherit the Crown and Royaltie: So if a Marquiss, or Duke have many Children, they are all Lords and Ladies, if they be lawfully, and in true Wedlock born, otherwise they are not: neither doth any more but one of the Legitimate Children inherit the Root, as to be Marquess or Duke, Dutchess or Marchioness: neither do the Daughters inherit, if there be Sons.

FIRST GENTLEMEN

But cannot a Dukes Daughter make her Husband a Prince?

SECOND GENTLEMEN

No, not except she hath the Inhereditary Honour: for if a Kings Daughter should marry a private Gentleman, he would remain as only in the Title of a Gentleman, unless the King did create a Title for him, or bestow a Title on him.

FIRST GENTLEMEN

Why? put case the Inhereditary Honour lay in the people, and they elect a King, hath that King no power to Create, or to give Honour?

SECOND GENTLEMEN

No, they may chuse Officers, but not give Titles, unless the people did dispossess themselves of their hereditary power, and give it to any man, and then the root of Honour lyes in him.

FIRST GENTLEMEN

Nor doth his Children receive no Titles from their Father?

SECOND GENTLEMEN

No, for the Title he hath, is none of his, he hath it but during life, unless the people will give a Lease, as for two or three Lives, yet they nominate those two or three Lives: So neither can they dispose of their Leases, or alter them, but at the peoples pleasure; like as those that are made Governors, they cannot dispose of their Governments to whom they please, as without the leave of those that placed them in the Government, neither do his Children receive any Titles therefrom; like as a Lord Mayor, his Son is not my Lord Mayor after him, unless he is made one; nor his children have no place by his Office, and an elective Prince, is but as a Lord Mayor, or rather like as a Deputy Governor, who as I said, may dispose of Places or Offices, but not give Dignities, Honours, or Titles.

FIRST GENTLEMEN

I thank you for your Information, for I was so ignorant, as I knew nothing of Heraldry.

[Exeunt.

SCENE XV

Enter **TWO GENTLEMEN**

FIRST GENTLEMEN

HAVE you seen the Imaginary Queen yet?

SECOND GENTLEMEN

What Imaginary Queen?

FIRST GENTLEMEN

Why a Great Queen, that every one goeth to kiss her hand.

SECOND GENTLEMEN

From what parts of the World came she?

FIRST GENTLEMEN

From the North parts.

SECOND GENTLEMEN
And doe so many go to kisse her hand?

FIRST GENTLEMEN
Yes, throngings of Common people.

SECOND GENTLEMEN
They would kiss the Dogs Tail if it were turned up and presented to them: but do any of the Nobles and Gentry kiss her hand?

FIRST GENTLEMEN
Some few that are newly come out of the Country to see sights in the City.

SECOND GENTLEMEN
Pish, in this Age there are so many of these kind of Bedlams, as I am weary to hear of them, as the Comical Dutchess, the Creating Princess, and the Created Prince, Prince Shaddow, and now the Imaginary Queen.

FIRST GENTLEMEN
Why Faith it is as good a sight as to see a Play.

SECOND GENTLEMEN
A puppet Play you mean; but the truth is, it is a disgrace to all noble persons, and great dignities, and true titles, to be thus mocked by imitators, it is a sign that all Europe is imbroiled in Wars so much as every one doth what they list.

FIRST GENTLEMEN
Why they are so far from being checkt or discountenanced for it, as there are many true Princes, great and noble persons as give the same respect and homage as if they were real Princes indeed and in truth.

SECOND GENTLEMEN
Then it if it were in my power I would divest those that had the right, and true dignities, and titles, and put them upon those that only acted princely and royal parts, since the Actors bear up so nobly, and the Spectators do creep and crouch so basely: but indeed both sides are Actors, both the Spectators and Players, only the one side Acts noble parts, the other side base parts, the one Acts the parts of Princes, the other of Servants; but I am sorrow to see True Honour wounded as it is.

FIRST GENTLEMEN
The truth of it is, True Honour lies a bleeding, and none doth offer to power in Balsimum.

[Exeunt.

SCENE XVI

Enter the Imaginary **QUEEN**, her **GENTLEMEN** Usher bare-headed leads her, her **PAGE** holds up her Train, her **WOMAN** follows her, and that is all her Train, a **COMPANY OF PEOPLE** flock to see her, and kneel to kiss her hand, she brideling in her Chin, as thinking that doth advance her state, they kneeling she gives them her hand to kiss, they pray God bless her Royalty, she nods them thanks, and then passes away.

FIRST WOMAN
Faith Neighbour methinks a Queen is not such a brave and glorious thing as I did imagine it.

SECOND WOMAN
I will tell you truly Neighbour, that if I had thought a Queen had been no finer a sight than this Queen is, I would have stayed in my house.

THIRD WOMAN
And so would I, I tell you truly Neighbour.

FOURTH WOMAN
I perceive Queens are no finer Creatures than other women are.

[Exeunt.

SCENE XVII

Enter **TWO GENTLEMEN**

FIRST GENTLEMEN
Lord what a ridiculous sight it is to see the Imaginary Queen act the part of Majesty?

SECOND GENTLEMEN
Faith she is so far from Majesty, as she cannot act the part, for she appears like a good Country Huswife.

FIRST GENTLEMEN
She is but a Gentlewoman, and that is all.

SECOND GENTLEMEN
We may see the difference of true Greatnesse, and that which is forced, there was the Queen Masculine; what a natural Majestie did she appear with? for all she had given up her Crown and Kingdome, yet her Royal Birth was seen in her Princely Carriage.

SECOND GENTLEMEN
It was a generous Act: But was it in her power to dispossesse her self of her natural Inheritance?

FIRST GENTLEMEN
It seems so; and it seems by her actions that she had rather see the World abroad, than rule a Kingdome at home, for she hath travelled most of all Europe over.

SECOND GENTLEMEN
She appears to be a Royal Lady.

[Exeunt.

SCENE XVIII

Enter **TWO** or **THREE** of the **COMICAL DUTCHESS'S WOMEN**, and **TWO** or **THREE BURGERS WIVES.**

FIRST WOMAN
The Comical Dutchess is brought to bed of the sweetest Princesse that ever was born.

FIRST WIFE
Indeed it is the sweetest Princesse that ever was born.

SECOND WIFE
We are glad, we hope her Highnesse will sleep well to night.

FIRST WIFE
Pray present our most humble and obedient duty to her Highnesse.

FIRST WOMAN
Will you not go in and see her, and kisse the young Princesses hand?

FIRST WIFE
If we may be so much honoured, we shall be very proud of that Grace and Honour.

SECOND WOMAN
Come, come, we will prefer you to that Grace and Favour.

[Exeunt.

SCENE XIX

Enter **TWO SCRIVENERS WIVES.**

FIRST WIFE
Welcome Mistriss Ink-pot, whether are you going so hastily?

SECOND WIFE
Truly Mistriss Paper, I am going to her Highness the Comical Dutchess, for I hear she is brought abed of a sweet young Princess.

FIRST WIFE
Is she so? I am glad her Highness pain is past, with all my heart.

SECOND WIFE

o am I, for now we shall have Dancing again, as soon as her Month is past.

FIRST WIFE

Yes, for she will send for us all, as soon as she is able to dance.

SECOND WIFE

Yes that she will, and give us all Favours to wear for her sake.

FIRST WIFE

But to some she gives her Picture too.

SECOND WIFE

Yes, but those she gives her Picture too, are of a higher Degree.

FIRST WIFE

By your favour, we are of as high a Degree as most that visit her.

SECOND WIFE

Yes, of the female Sex, but not of the Masculine Sex; for there are great Persons that visit her.

FIRST WIFE

Very few, but only of the Red Oker Nation, or some Strangers that are Travellers, that visit her, as they pass other waies, else the men that visit her, are of as inferior degree as we, as Fidlers, Dancers, Players, and the like.

SECOND WIFE

By your favour, there are sometimes Burgers and Gentlemen.

FIRST WIFE

Yes sometimes, when she sends for to invite them to dance, or intreats them to come and visit her; and then she presents them with her Colours.

[Exeunt.

SCENE XX

Enter the **LADY TRUE HONOUR**, and **MADAM INQUIRER**.

MADAM INQUIRER

Lord, Madam, I was ask'd to day, why your Honour doth not visit the Comical Dutchess, nor the Imaginary Queen?

LADY TRUE HONOUR

Why, should I that am Intituled with True Honour, and Princely Dignity, which Titles were created from an Absolute and Divine Power, give place to mock Honours, and feigned Dignities? shall Princes in Royal Courts, give place to Princes in Playes?

MADAM INQUIRER
But every one doth not rightly understand a Princely Dignity.

LADY TRUE HONOUR
I will instruct you in the degrees of Princes, and their derivation; but first, let me tell you, the Princely Arms, or Seal, is a Crown; for a Crown is the General Arms, or Seal of all Princely Dignities, and every degree is known and distinguished by the several fashions of their Crowns; for a Vicounts Crown, which is the first degree of a Prince, is not like the Earls Crown, which is the second degree; nor an Earls Crown is not like a Marquisses Crown, which is the third degree; that is, there is some difference in the Crown; nor a Marquisses Crown is not like a Dukes Crown, which is the fourth degree; nor a Dukes Crown is not like a close Imperial Crown, which is the last and highest degree; that is, there is some difference in the Crown of each degree: Now there are Absolute Princes, Tributary, and Subject Princes, but none can be wholly call'd Absolute Princes, but those that have the Imperial Crown, which are Absolute Kings and Emperors, being the only chosen of God, and by that the only Creators of Titles; for they only are the Fountain, or Springs of Honour.

MADAM INQUIRER
How comes it that Subjects are made Princes?

LADY TRUE HONOUR
By Adoption: for all Subject Princes are Princes by Adoption: that is, they are adopted to their Princely Dignity, so that by Adoption, they are the Cosens to Royaltie, and are called by their Soveraigns, Kings Cosens, and are adorn'd with Royal Robï¿½s, indued with Royal Power, and observed with Royal Ceremony, and are allowed some Customs and Imposts out of the Revenue of the Kingdom, and many privileges which belong to the Princely Dignities: Thus Kings call their Subject Princes, Cosens, as being adopted to their Princely Royaltie, like as all Absolute Monarchs call each other Brother, as in relation to each others Royalty: and being all of them Gods annointed, and appointed Deputies on Earth, for Government and Honour, they are the sacred Magistrates of God, the divine Fountains of Honour: Thus true Honour is derived from Heaven, and ought to be respected, and bowed too, as being divine: but in this age Honour is used, or abused, as other divine things are: this is the reason I will not visit the Apocriphal Ladies: for my Honour is derived from the sacred Spring of Honour, and is not a self-given Honour and Dignity, which ought to be punished as a Presumption and Usurpation: but I have so much Honour, as not to abase the Honour and Dignity that my Husband, and his Fore-fathers were adopted too: And I by Marriage, being one with my Husband; for man and wife are but one, and my Husbands Honour being Inhereditary, succeeds to his Children; wherefore his Wife will never give place to Mountebanks.

MADAM INQUIRER
Indeed the strange ridiculousness, and folly, and mad presumption is, that the Apocriphal Ladies take more State, or at least as much as sacred Royaltie.

LADY TRUE HONOUR
But if Royaltie will suffer such Heresies, and Hereticks in the Court of Honour, they are not to be lamented, if their Courts fall to utter ruine; for it is with Titles and Dignities, as with Laws; if there were

no Laws, there would be no Government, and if there were no Degrees and dignities, there would be no Royalty; so likewise if the Laws be corrupt and abused, Governwent will fall to ruin, and if Honour be abused and usurpt, Royaltie will fall from its Throne; but howsoever, I keep up the Right of my place, because it is the cause and interest of all the Nobility of my Country, so that if I should give place, I should be a Traytor to true Honour, and dignified Persons.

SCENE XXI

Enter **TWO WOMEN** of the Comical Dutchess.

FIRST WOMAN
Well, now the Duke of Inconstancy hath forsaken our Lady, his Comical Dutchess, all our State must down.

SECOND WOMAN
Yes, and we must lose our places, in going before others, as being Dutchess's women.

FIRST WOMAN
The Dutchess cryed all night.

SECOND WOMAN
She had no more reason to cry, than she had, for the matter of Dignity; for, pray consider, her Highness may keep the same State, as being Dutchess still, as well as she did before; for she possess'd the Honour no more than she doth now, and so now no less than she did then.

FIRST WOMAN
That is true, but the Duke did help to countenance her State, so long as he did live with her, as a Husband, whereas now she will be hist off the Stage.

SECOND WOMAN
Faith Confidence, and a Resolution will bear her up, wherefore let us perswade her not to be daunted, or put out of countenance, and she having the same Estate she had, may maintain her self as high as she hath done.

FIRST WOMAN
You say true, and the flanting shew will dazle the eyes, and delude the understanding of the Spectators.

FIRST WOMAN
Yes, of the Vulgar.

[Exeunt

SCENE XXII

Enter **TWO GENTLEMEN**

FIRST GENTLEMEN
HONOUR goes a begging.

SECOND GENTLEMEN
Why?

FIRST GENTLEMEN
Why there is an Ale Wife made a Countesse.

SECOND GENTLEMEN
As how?

FIRST GENTLEMEN
Why the Earl Undone hath married Mistriss Tip-tape.

SECOND GENTLEMEN
But he hath a Wife living.

FIRST GENTLEMEN
That is all one, for did not the Duke of Inconstancy marry a Lady, and made her a Dutchess, although he had a Dutchess to his Wife before, by whom he was a Duke.

SECOND GENTLEMEN
I perceive Great Noble Persons may do what they will: for if a poor mean man should have two Wives at one time, they would be surely punished; nay, in some Kingdoms they would be hanged.

[Exeunt.

SCENE XXIII

Enter **TWO SCRIVENERS WIVES**

FIRST WIFE
DO you hear that the Duke of Inconstancy hath forsaken his Comical Dutchess?

SECOND WIFE
Yes, but that is nothing.

FIRST WIFE
Have you been with her Highness since?

SECOND WIFE
Yes.

FIRST WIFE

And how looks she upon her misfortunes?

SECOND WIFE

Why she appears the same, and keeps greater State than ever she did; yea, even her Children are served more royally than ever.

FIRST WIFE

Faith she is to be commended, if it will hold out.

SECOND WIFE

As long as she hath money, it will hold.

FIRST WIFE

O, money doth all things.

[Exeunt.

MARGARET CAVENDISH – A CONCISE BIBLIOGRAPHY

Philosophical Fancies (1653)
Poems and Fancies (1653)
Philosophical and Physical Opinions (1655)
Nature's Pictures drawn by Fancie's Pencil to the Life (1656)
The World's Olio (1655)
Playes, (1662) folio, containing twenty-one plays including
Loves Adventures
The Several Wits
Youths Glory, and Deaths Banquet
The Lady Contemplation
Wits Cabal
The Unnatural Tragedy
The Public Wooing
The Matrimonial Trouble
Nature's Three Daughters (Beauty, Love and Wit) Part I & Part II
The Religious
The Comical Hash
Bell in Campo
A Comedy of the Apocryphal Ladies
The Female Academy
Plays never before printed (1668), containing five plays.
The Sociable Companions, or the Female Wits
The Presence
The Bridals
The Convent of Pleasure
A Piece of a Play

Orations of Divers Sorts (1662)
Philosophical Letters, or Modest Reflections upon some Opinions in Natural Philosophy maintained by several learned authors of the age (1664)
CCXI Sociable Letters (1664)
Observations upon Experimental Philosophy & Description of a New World (1666)
The Blazing World (1666)
The Life of William Cavendish, Duke, Marquis, and Earl of Newcastle, Earl of Ogle, Viscount Mansfield, and Baron of Bolsover, of Ogle, Bothal, and Hepple, &c. (1667)
Grounds of Natural Philosophy (1668)